modern absurdity

collected & selected poems

Joseph Fulkerson

First edition

ISBN: 979-8-9873315-1-4

published by Laughing Ronin Press 2023

Acknowledgements

Many thanks to the following Editors who originally published these now out of print collections: Marc Brüseke-Analog Submission Press, Tohm Bakelas-Between Shadows Press, Jacob Louis Beaney-Hickathrift Press

Contents

STONKS!

The experts are convinced
it's a bull market
or maybe a bear market
either way
they're certain it's a mammal
with four legs, possibly hooves
but to be safe
they're not ruling out claws.

They are convinced
trickle-down economics does work
but only if you have a white collar

-or-

if you've ever attended a
three martini lunch meeting
even more so if you can

write it off as a business expense.

Choosing to buy into this
provides a guarantee of residual income
& a lifetime of resentment
& complacency.

The fix is in;
I'd be remiss if I didn't state the obvious.

A metric shit-ton of regret is in store for
you, mister.

You can't deny
the devil has the best deal
when it comes to plea deals.

He'll get you prime real-estate
on the 9th green of the
9th circle.

You'll be a scapegoat
the fall guy
caught red-handed
holding a red herring.

You'll be first in line for an ass-whooping
& last in line for your parole hearing.

If the road to hell is paved with
good intentions, then the road to heaven
is littered with anal fissures.

The saying goes "if you mess with the bull
you get the horns."

They failed to mention the bull cock.

You're prime ass, prime meat

in prime time

delicate sensibilities are a delicacy

in the prison yard.

You'll be sewing golden parachutes

into white collars

in your sleep

in no time.

It's a bull market after all.

Or was it bear?

LUCK FAVORS the RISK takers

although

    I'll venture

a guess

      the corpse

at

the

bottom

of the chasm

    would disagree with that statement

WRONG IN ALL THE RIGHT PLACES

People claim they want honesty
but they're scared of the truth.
They want advice without an opinion.

They want their courage tested
without the struggle
associated with it.

They want patience
& they want it now!

They want talent
yet are unwilling to put in the work
necessary to bring it forth.
It hurts wrong in all the right places.

I 🩶 TYLER

Doive?

Duvet?

What's the difference

it's a fucking blanket.

snout chasing tail

Can you understand the desperation
of the inner self?

Can you empathize with the plight
of a man who has no direction or plan?

Will you sympathize with the man
helping to circumvent
the upcoming storm of the soul?

Who can understand this?

It is beyond interpretation
or even comprehension.

My emotions play on an endless loop

snout chasing tail

on a lifelong journey

to the depths of utter contempt

& disdain.

My pen flows as a broken waterspout

pouring onto the page, flooding the world

with my words.

My thoughts many

yet answers are few

meditating thoroughly

but speaking sparingly.

I am forever lost

in the desert of my mind.

TO MY FORMER SELF, FROM A FUTURE ITERATION

You should write this down.
Actually, you should write
everything down
all the time.

On Oct 12th, 2022
at approximately 5:30pm
when you get to Jimmy John's
order the *Beach Club* instead
of the *Totally Tuna*. You'll be
glad you did.

Don't stop by the bank to withdraw
cash from the ATM. It will eat your card,
forcing you to use your MasterCard

the rest of the week.

Instead of meeting Matt
to have a drink, stay home.

If you absolutely **insist** on going
don't stay out too late.
10:30-11pm at the latest.

When you get to the pub
sit at the fifth barstool from the door.
The one directly in front of the taps.

At exactly 8:35pm order an old-fashioned
with Jameson & sip until gone
ignoring the girl with the nose ring
who's new to town.
You'll thank me later.

Just enjoy the karaoke

& have another drink

or two, if you like.

Now whatever you do, do not

make eye contact with the woman

directly behind you at your 5 o'clock.

Don't watch as she takes a drink

& laughs with that blonde friend

of hers, all the while making sure

you're paying attention

 out of her peripherals.

DO NOT engage in small talk.

As a matter of fact, don't talk

to anyone at all.

If you do, you will find her

witty & funny & sexy as hell.

Resist.

You will know her voice

like the melody to a song

you can't quite remember

but that you never want to forget.

Please, please don't give her your number.

Resist looking into her hazel-colored eyes

try not to fall in love

with the way she bites her bottom lip

while thinking of an excuse

to come back up to the bar.

She'll find one, & make her way

back to where you sit.

She will be everything we've been looking for.
Everything we need.

We will fall in love with her instantly.
We will propose quickly
get married quicker
& live a happy life
for a long time, that is
until the cancer takes her from us.

It will be the hardest thing
we will ever encounter.

You will consider death to be easier
& I'm not so sure it wasn't
                              -isn't-
which is the reason for this
highly irregular correspondence.

So do us both a favor—

don't go to karaoke night on

Thursday October 12th, 2022.

It's too much of a loss.

Stay home & watch **Broad City** instead.

(this week's episode is quite funny)

You will thank me later.

Sincerely,

Future Iteration of Us

debutant

You're a miracle of debauchery

a debutant

a fuck boi

they're lining up

begging you

to grab them by the pussy

you're a rapscallion

a trailblazer

a ram scaling the crags

up the side of the mountain

a trendsetter

a taste maker, king maker

a bellwether &

a broke-dick bloat

of a bloke.

Good riddance,

Agent Orange

the space between

There is a difference
between education & experience
motivation & dedication
understanding & enlightenment.

Although often confused
one for the other
the space between is vast
immeasurable even.

Both Buddhist & Christian
Muslim & Hindu
Jew & Hari Krishna
all believe in a higher power—
a mother

a father, a deity

their paths to enlightenment
to salvation
        Nirvana
are as varied & conflicted
as the cluster of stars in the heavens.

the united states of
dichotomy

We are urban playgrounds

& rural homesteads

We are inner city concrete jungles

& rolling Appalachian hills

We are Wall Street

Main Street

A backcountry road

With the windows down

Come one, come all

But

We are building this wall

We are the abused

We perpetrate abuse

We are predators

& the prey

We are instigators

Propagators

A tourniquet

On the arm of justice

We are innocent

We are the accused

We are propaganda

We are fake news

We've made an institution
Out of infatuation with half-truths

We are the privileged
As well as the underrepresented

We are white privilege

We are the gentrification of all

We are law enforcement

We are racial profiling
We are *stop & frisk*
We are discrimination

We are a *no-knock warrant*
To the wrong apartment

We are the protester

& the establishment

Which is protested against

We are unrest & upheaval in the streets

We are the distilled will of the masses

We are legion

We are the upper class

The lower class

& everything in-between

We are the middle child

The only child

The chosen

&

Lost generation

We are first generation

Second & third

Generation citizenship

We are the perpetrator

& the arbitrator

Of justice & injustice

We are jihad realized

Sadism exemplified

Unmitigated terror

The wager of wars

We are the land of opportunity

& mistakes

We are rising to the challenge

We are the envy of many a nation

The balm of Gilead
We are democracy

We are more than the sum of our parts
We lead by example

We are hope & optimism
We are free & fair

We are stand up
& be counted
For what we believe in

We are neighbor

Helping neighbor

We are

Bipartisanship

Biracial

Bisexual

Bilingual

Nondenominational

Multicultural

&

By the way

We are on the verge of something great

If we could just get out of our own way.

wad of flesh

What are we

but a spark of consciousness

                    encased in a wad of flesh

walking around bumping

into one another?

LOST In tRanSLation

in transit

wide-eyed stares

blank expressionless faces

shifting eyes foretelling the incapacity

to relate to the poured-out souls

of the next generation

buildings abandoned, condemned

housing projects, playgrounds

rusted into non-existence

we all share the blame

for this generation's

refusal to grow up.

More accurately

their inability

to break through the confines

of adolescence & become

the torchbearers

we all need them to be.

the mechanism

A pearl starts as

an irritant to the oyster.

It's the oyster's triggered response

that creates this object of beauty.

A diamond is created

under extremes of

temperature & pressure

which over time results

in the hardest stone known to man.

Suffering is the mechanism

the catalyst

for inspiration

for in the balance
of suffering's scales
all of life is weighed.

Successes, failures
good & not so good choices
all more poignant when viewed
through its lens.

Genuine, unadulterated suffering
most of us will never know
yet often that is what
separates the mundane
from the divine.

Death comes on twelve wings

The botched second coming

of the tentacle-clad monolith

                descended

from the brothel in the clouds

like a child's discarded plaything

its innards exposed

for the world to see.

Multitudes dying

cancerous deaths

tapeworm filled vomit

venom sac lungs

ending our cradle death

with a raspy air of finality.

An absentee father on bedrest

is exposed to all sorts of chemicals

straight from the needle's dripping stem.

Don't make liars out of us, Daddy.

You always were the one to choose

which life to take next.

Knife wounds never heal as they should

edge jags to edge, unhealed flesh

puckering away from itself

in stubborn refusal.

The switchblade cuts

to the bone quick

blood geysers dance

to the rhythm of the heartbeat

arterial sprays warming

the aching gullet

of my lecherous mouth.

Then there's no stopping my lust.

Therapeutic isolation is

the only way to do it.

No love lost as they say.

I've become the harbinger

of dismay, the calculated risk

that you're willing to stomach

I am the relaxed sphincter

on fresh roadkill

I am the putrid smell

wafting from the closet

where your skeletons reside

I am the tickle in the back

of your throat

& the bad taste

in your mouth

both the allergen

& the antihistamine

I am the word on the tip of the tongue

the thinly veiled threat

I am the mistakes you wish to forget

bastards of an unplanned family

we always wanted

but never could ask for.

All that's left is a kid
face flecked with dirt
staring at the ruddy complexion
of his guardian angel reflected
in the pool of blood.

Blue lights flashing a disco inferno
gives the desired attention
but at what cost?

The gallows cast a long shadow.

the collective narrative

In times like these
a man finds himself clinging
to familiar things for comfort.

The economy is in the crapper
there's a worldwide pandemic
tearing through the streets

& when I sit down to write
I just end up staring at this blank page.

There are things to be said, dammit!

Yet here I sit pondering my dedication
to the word, second guessing
my resolve to do more than exist

to be more than a cog in the machine

to add a page

a chapter, dare I say

an entire book to the collective

narrative of humanity.

VOLCANO TEARS

A tear falls

from the cheek of a volcano

                              scorching the earth

searing its emotions

into the footprint of history

PRIORITIES today are as FOLLOWS:

[ ] Milk the cow, but take care to be gentle with the udders (you know how she gets)

[ ] Wash the comforter & sheets-make sure & dry them twice

[ ] Go to grocery-get bananas (the organic kind)

[ ] Pay your mortgage-because you know, foreclosure is a bad thing

[ ] Iron your shirt-dress for the job you want

[ ] Smile & wave

[ ] Be kind, please rewind

[ ] Vacuum the floors-cleanliness is next to godliness

A MERRY-GO-ROUND IN PURGATORY

Philosophical   Theological   Economical
Detrimental   Emotional   Spiritual   Eventual
Irrational
     Occasionally regretful

All words that describe the feelings
I have on a daily basis.

I go from contemplating the mysteries
of the universe, to recounting the most useless
of information, trivial at best.

Such are the cycles of thought

that flow through the mind

on an endless loop

like a merry-go-round

in purgatory.

screaming into the night

Sometimes

writing feels like

screaming into

the black of night

with a bullhorn

other times

it feels like

whispering a secret

into the ear

of your sweetheart

      -either way-

words are strung together

to form sentences

which form paragraphs

& chapters

in much the same way

they always have

but on the rare occasion

when the stars align

& the muse takes pity

new & exciting ways

are found

to say those things

which cannot be

easily expressed

& that is what

keeps me

coming back

to the page.

the withered prince

The face of the withering prince
racked with grief, losses stacking
end over end

multiplying the heartache of
a thousand martyrs
a midlife crisis developing
while we wait

letters crossing continents to find
you lacking, fingers cascading over
the quivering comely parts of another

ecstatic asphyxiation closing tracheal
pathways, bruised with passion
purple & throbbing member

gaining entrance to your fallow earth

elation spewing forth my seed
sown wildly in vain
aching for the gap between us,
between you

swallowing the tonic
I succumb to the bitterness
of complacency.

Never the one to write a eulogy
I feign heartache & tackle the enormity
of my fickle cell anemia,
cells dividing unto senescence.

Seizing the opportunity
I lunge into the abyss

a mere wraith of my former self

alone to the reaches of

Death's scythe.

sweet symphony

Creativity is birthed

from the tumult of restlessness

buried deep down in the soul.

It is formed from the shifting

of the tectonic plates within

from the friction of life

rubbing hard against it.

That rubbing together

the abrasiveness of the process

churns out the sweet symphony

of the written word.

JWFII

I am a middle child

the only son

two weeks late

for my own birthday

I am riding my bike

through the neighborhood

all day long

I am speed runs of Super Mario Bros

on long summer days

I am passing out Bible tracts

instead of dressing up

or receiving candy on Halloween

I am weeklong tent revivals

in the sweltering Kentucky heat

I am the homeschooled middle school blues

I am too proud to wear hand-me-downs

but too poor to pass them up

I am awkward lovemaking

on the bench seat

of my 85' Chevy S-10

at the drive-in theater

I am naivety & heartache

    I am Toni Braxton's *Never gonna love*

again

I am the mended pieces of a broken heart

I am nursed back to health
with the help of my friends

I am R. Kelly's *Ignition the remix*
                    engine raring to go

I am a dumbstruck, love-sick puppy
lost in the unexplored galaxies
that lie within her eyes

I am a newlywed honeymooning
on the wings of angels

I am a proud new father, scared
out of his wits
I am sleepless nights & hazy days

I am weeks

& months

& years removed

                    yet

I am restless & unhappy

longing for something else

I am both the cheated on

as well as the cheater

I am divorce & despair

I am all-night sobbing

I am Toni Braxton's *Never gonna love again*

                                    again

I am nursed back to health

with sadness & copious

amounts of alcohol

I am R. Kelly's *Ignition the remix*

back in the saddle

once more

I am Joseph 2.0

I am let the pregame begin

the life of the party

I Am the after party

I am 3am breakfast at Denny's

& early morning drunk sex

I am the flavor of the month

I am weeks

& months

& many lovers removed

I am jaded & cynical

& just plain lonely

I am long goodbyes

& starting over

I am cautious optimism

personified

I am hard-earned wisdom

Exemplified

I am more than the sum of my parts

I am an amalgam of successes

& failures

but mostly failures

&

Still here.

Still restless.

Longing for something else.

Honeybee Honey-Do

If I could be

the one

you love

I'd be

a honeybee.

I'd make

a beeline

over

to you

seeking out

the sweet nectar

within your petals

diving in headfirst

swallowing all I can

filling up

my little

bee pockets

as I went.

Then

I would

hurry back

to the hive

& busy myself

transforming

our love

into a

lifetime supply

of honey.

night shift at the aluminum factory

There are people
who've worked here
their entire career
        or rather
who have made
entire careers
out of not working

so
I don't feel
too bad for
taking the time
to write this poem.

chic-o-stick

once as kids

my sisters & I

walked

with my dad

to the local IGA

to buy a pack

of cigarettes.

He let us each

pick out

a small piece

of candy

&

after much deliberation

I settled on a

chic-O-stick—

a toasted

peanut butter

& coconut log

of crunchy goodness.

On the walk back

I was

completely transfixed

by the taste,

happy with

the universe

& my place

in it.

I bought one

the other day,

quite a bit smaller

& more expensive

than I remember

but it instantly

took me back

to that day

& time in my life

& what I wouldn't give

to be on

that walkabout

with my dad

& sisters again

nothing

to worry about

or to focus on

save

the savory

sweetness

of my

peanut butter log.

dotdotdot

the ellipsis

as it's called

is used for

all the things

we want

to say

but are

unable to

for

the moments

we can't

      shouldn't

say anything

at all

especially

reserved

for those

3 a.m.

conversations

the ones

better left

unsaid

those

you wish you

could

take back

in the sober

light of

the

following

day

never mind

The

first rule

    of fight club is...

           oh shit

I already fucked it up.

WORK IN PROGRESS

I'm ~~not mad~~ can't be mad

at you anymore.

I understand perfectly.

You're ~~scared~~ *terrified*

to be alone, of

being rejected

& ~~unwilling~~ unable

to put

someone else

before yourself.

You see

you *can't* be blamed

because you are

bereft of

any character

that would

drive you

to be selfless

& I can no longer

blame you

because

to ~~blame you~~ <u>do so</u>

means

I place an expectation

on you.

One that believes

if given

the chance

you would

choose

differently

& give me

the opportunity

to

choose for myself.

I know that

to be

~~a farce.~~ <u>an illusion.</u>

You've shown

your

true colors.

You're ~~compromised.~~ ~~defiled.~~ <u>morally</u>

<u>bankrupt,</u>

Just

an empty, soulless

self-serving

husk

walking around

pretending

to be

a good person.

StFU

she's partial to the destitute

the downtrodden

the forgotten

the misfits, miscreants

& losers

the hungover hangdogs

      those

desperate for answers

usually

on a bar stool

or sitting

in all-night diners

intoxicated by drink

& conversation

or

stumbling down

midnight streets

howling at the moon

like mad men

& women

or

on a lonely park bench

watching the sun

rise

on another hopeless day

there

she waits patiently

to impart

her secrets

whisper her truths

to us

If only

we'll

STFU

long enough

to listen

steady as she goes

Rise & shine

part your hair on the left

make sure to brush & floss

no cavities will be tolerated,

don't want to get the dreaded

-GINGIVITIS-

hide your tattoos

tuck in your shirt

& stop slouching

eat your greens

do your homework

pay your taxes

go to church

get married & settle down

your upside-down mortgage

notwithstanding

the kiddos will need a college fund, don't

forget the employer-matched 401k up to 6%

embrace the two-party system

your choices being

-either-

-or-

it's the same choice regardless

death by a thousand cuts, or

a thousand little compromises

don't rock the boat

keep one foot in front of the other

being careful not to say anything too

progressive

too conservative

wouldn't want to make waves

to cause anyone to feel uncomfortable

it would be a shame to tarnish

your spotless record

of having nothing to add

of never weighing in

right down the middle

keep it between the lines

you can't hold an opinion

so controversial

as to upset the order of things

people may think you've gone

& taken a side

you need to keep them guessing

as to what you stand for

if anything at all.

Once as a young boy

there were two girls

both named Sarah

they called me on the telephone

asking which one I liked the best.

      They told me I had to choose.

Make one girl happy

make one cry—

I was damned either way.

So, I chose

& have been choosing

the wrong Sarah

ever since.

HUNTING GROUNDS

I saw you today & froze

with that-*deer in the headlights*

of a speeding car-stare.

You didn't see me, so it wasn't

permanent, although the scars

threatened to reopen & fester

at the mere thought of you.

I look at you & want to play

a game of hopscotch in oncoming traffic.

I'm hoping to change that soon.

I hear freeze tag is a better alternative.

It hurts less when you're sent careening

through the air smashing into things

like speed limit signs or mile markers

than the reality that you've moved

on & we're through.

I want to terraform the landscape

of your heart, which as of yet remains

unsuitable for any long-term growth.

I know the future makes the past

seem vaguely familiar, but

I don't want to be a carcinogen

to your pulmonary functions any longer.

We lost quite a bit in the last one

it still feels like today's news,

but that's just me reading too much

into the situation again.

Feelings always were optional for you
while mine were free for the taking.

I don't know how to try anymore.
It ends up being a ten-car pileup
during a blinding snowstorm.

Won't it be the same as last time?

Remember calling me an asshole
in front of that bar full of strangers?

They believed everything you told
them, although I must admit you
did put on quite the performance.

I wish it had gone differently.

I would've conceded that you were right

-I was being an asshole-

that you were justified

in all your anger

& we would've gone on

with the night still believing

we were meant for each other.

It went differently as you know

& I'm left with the tapestry

of what was left unsaid, undone

by our silence.

We never cleared the air between us

the only oxygen in the room turning toxic

poisoning any future civilizations that may

have come from all those sleepless nights

& endless conversations into the wee
hours of the morning.

You needed more, I offered less.
Then you gave me less when I needed more.

You sat on the kitchen floor crying
head in hands, our unwillingness
to change an apparition that haunts
us both to this day.

What was so important that we
undressed each other so completely,
dismantling the very fabric of what
brought us together in the first place?

I would've crossed continents to see you

weathering different time zones,

you being the one truth left to die in me.

In the end we were left with knuckles

scraped clean to the bone

and us both worse for the wear.

You & I,

both predator & prey

drawn to the same body of water

on the Saharan plains

an unlikely alliance

a shaky truce

but for a moment

   then

incisor to throat muscle

arterial tears geyser red

separating sinew from bone.

You can't blame the lioness

for being a lioness.

Her nature cannot be denied.

She must hunt.

She must feed.

She must mate.

Hunt. Feed. Mate. Repeat.

you got moxy, kid!

As a writer, or as in any noble pursuit

from time to time, you find yourself

at a point of desperation.

Which is not a bad place to be

creatively speaking.

On the contrary, being within

these confines seem to activate

a whole new skillset for the individual.

It'll make you think differently.

It'll make you do abnormal things.

You'll do what you need to do,

say what would normally go unspoken.

You'll say what you feel.

For the stark reality is

desperation doesn't give a shit.

Desperation is the divorced child

of opportunity & talent.

The bastard child of restlessness

& hopelessness.

If desperation were a house,

it would be a single-story ranch

on the corner of **Impossible Way**

& **No Choice Loop**.

Desperation finds a way

because there's no other choice.

It doesn't care what it looks like

sounds like, tastes

or smells like.

It prefers to work alone, but at times

you will find it in amongst its friends

Chance & *Luck*.

It doesn't care about anything

but doing the deed.

Desperation rolls up its sleeves

pushes talent aside

& does it it's damn self.

It seeks out the *how* & *where*

& says fuck the *why*.

It cares very little about your

inconvenience or your opinion

for that matter.

It pinches its nose, grabs a shovel

& scoops up the steaming pile.

If there isn't a shovel

it will pick up great big handfuls

of it & hurl it in

everyone's smug little faces.

It doesn't care.

It doesn't give a flying fuck.

It takes to the streets

& demands to be heard.

It will march all the way

down main street

to the steps of city hall

to get it done,

Grassroots style.

It'll kick in the door

snatch you out of bed

& drag you by the ankles

kicking & screaming into the night.

It's relentless.

Desperation will either make a fool

or a hero out of you-

your choice.

There's a razor's edge

of a difference anyway.

It will either get down on one knee

to propose

or leave you bruised & bleeding

in the gutter, wrists bound with electrical tape.

Any given day of the week

in every city of the world

you can watch it play out.

Desperation is the single mom

working three jobs to keep the lights on.

It's what sends the unemployed dad

out of state looking for work.

It's what makes the quiet kid

stand up to the bully-

fists clenched; knuckles scraped.

It's in the eyes of the wrongly accused

& wrongly incarcerated.

It's on the lips & faces of those

who can't stand another 12-hour shift

another soulless, bone-grinding week of menial work

affording only a meager existence.

It fills the bars on Saturday night

& the church pews on Sunday morning,

& sometimes

it is hard to tell the difference

between the two.

It's better for a man

to stomach failure

than to die with regret.

Pay attention to the man

who has a limp in his walk

& a tremble in his talk,

for that man has wrestled with

success & failure

& his body bears the

scars to prove it.

He's searched

the alleyways & bars,

roamed the midnight streets

howling to the muse for inspiration

& cursing the night

for giving in to the sunrise

of a meaningless new day.

the lifespan of a successful failure

More & more I feel like I am hurtling

towards a vast expanse of nothingness.

Like I'm late for a date with no one

or nothing in particular,

but late all the same.

I'm a hungover hangdog

a misfiring misfit

grasping at signs of life

in a last-ditch effort

to feel something real.

I'm a genuine wino

a whining fake

& a successful failure

of a human being.

Considered a success by society's

standards, but a sellout to the man

& to compromise & cowardice.

I'm a burnt-up burnout,

sleepwalking through life

with the understanding it may

all end with a whimper.

A husk of a man

with lofty goals, yes

but no drive left

at the end of the day.

One who's spent all his time

& energy on the wrong people

at the wrong time.

I've used up all my youth

on the hustle

on chasing the dream

whatever the fuck

that could be.

What's left is a half-wit has-been

masquerading as a man with a plan.

A wife, two kids

& a pension that likely won't

be there when I need it.

Every day is a lonely slog.

But when I sit down to write

the Muse is there

& she tells me things

some things I know

& some I don't

but I listen all the same.

Sometimes she says nothing at all

so, we just sit there together

as the jazz plays

& the whiskey goes down

smoother with every drink

it's good

& I start to feel better about things,

like maybe it's not all piss & shit after all.

there was supposed to be cake

I remember you!

Young, carefree

ten foot tall

& bulletproof

too full of adventure

to settle for mediocrity.

Dizzy

with life's possibilities

you jumped

whole-heartedly

into the possibilities

of the future

      ready

for whatever

life threw at you

& boy

did it throw you

a curveball

with a dash of pepper.

You searched

for more than

a menial

existence for

meager

compensation.

You were led

to believe

there would be

someone, something

waiting

for you

at the finish line.

Instead

you were beat-

down & threatened

for pursuing

your dreams

swiftly

kicked out

into the world

to find your way-

any way

will do.

Your insides

began to rot

limbs suffered

atrophy waiting

for something

to happen.

Disillusionment setting in,

you settled for

what was within

reach.

Congratulations

you've become

~~a contributing member~~

~~of society.~~ <u>a battery source</u>

<u>for the capitalist machine.</u>

check & mate

I was folding laundry

the other day

when it struck me.

"Why am I the only one

in this house who washes

the towels?" I asked. "Why don't you?"

"Because you just do it," she said.

"Well hell," I said, & went back

to folding.

Asleep at the Wheel

It feels

as though

something has broken

inside me.

I lead a life of quiet desperation.

I want to clear the air

with my screams.

Deplete the oxygen completely.

I was supposed to be something by now.

How do you abandon all hope?

One foot

in front of the other.

We all thought we would

conquer the world

that we would be witness

to the magnitude

or see the birth

of some great discovery

that the universe

would willingly give up

her secrets, just because

we had the courage to ask.

Sadly, that's not how it played out.

Our lives have become

a celebration of mediocrity

documenting

every facet

in excruciating detail

recounting

the minutiae of

our days to complete

strangers

chasing likes

& posting status updates

as if it were

of the utmost

importance

responding to

most conversations

with emojis

& Hashtags.

What Hashtag best describes your life?

#asleepatthewheel

my bad

I feel too deep

take

too long

to forgive

        to make decisions

I ask too few questions

& give too many answers

I believe too much

in completely random things

while doubting simple facts

I don't expect much

out of others

while asking

too much of myself

I live in the shadow

of my shortcomings

which tower

       endlessly

over me

I've made an entire ecosystem

out of denial

having the ability

yet lacking the discipline

to follow through

with the simplest

of tasks

don't ask me how

or why I'm here

I was looking for a way out

of the mundanity

of my existence

which

up to this point

excluded your judgment

& the subsequent

justification

of my actions

catch-up

My life has been

a succession

of fits

& starts

a tinder box of regret

& missed opportunities

chances

unwilling to take

mistakes

unwilling to make

all set to go up

in a conflagration of flames.

Just when I thought
I had it all figured out
they change the rules

moving the goal line
further away
with each
rushing yard.

Any progress made
pales
in comparison
to others.

I was behind
at birth
& have been

playing *catch-up*

ever since.

When I get to the end

will I see

the finish line?

Will there be

a crowd gathered

to cheer my spent effort?

chad

for Craig

On the jobsite

you were the one

who liked to draw dicks

of all shapes & sizes

hairy or manscaped

veiny or wrinkled

in the most random places.

I remember

climbing down into

the turbine housing

& under the decking

to get to a junction box

& there

next to it

was a

detailed drawing

of a penis.

The next one I saw

was a stubby little prick

drawn on the

Porta John wall.

They started showing

up everywhere after that.

Seeing those doodles

in the most random of places

always made me

smile.

It let me know

if only briefly

that I wasn't alone.

That you had been there too.

If only someone

had been there

for you.

So

the next time

I see a cloud

that looks

dangerously close

to the shape of a penis

I'll just laugh

knowing you

traded in

your sharpie

for a set of wings.

Rest easy my friend.

PENINSULA

the saying goes

"no man is an island..."

but fuck it all

if I don't feel

at least

like

a peninsula

out of time

I am a man who doesn't fit

       out of time

       out of place

I need to get back

to where I belong

alone all the time

alone in a

crowded room

surrounded by

multitudes

       damn the people

the masses

sucking air

through wide open

holes where mouths

should be

blank expressionless slits

for eyes

we're ripe for

an apocalypse

      The end is nigh!

the signs are everywhere

Repent!

    Repent!

The kingdom of God is at hand!

Weeping

& gnashing of teeth

will soon follow!

cultishly happy

justifying the mediocrity in others

         to validate mine

    celebrating conformity

    because

I'm terrified

    of my own compromise

overheard conversations in the south #37

"Will you do a Vegas-bomb with me?"

"Nah, bitch that's what killed Mamaw!"

tRACKING PATTERNS

I find the limits in people daily
if not hourly

no one can give me
what I need
what I crave

Can anyone know me?
Does anyone have-lying
on the hallway floor crying-
thoughts about me?

Does anyone really see me?
my successes
my failures

pains

ambitions

fears

hopes & dreams

Is there anyone

willing to trace their fingers

along the divots in my soul

tracking patterns

the pain took,

skin puckering away

from the wound's exit?

Do they see the cracks in my smile

or the tears-stained cheeks

behind the mask? *Can it even be called a mask*

at this point?

I've worn it so long

it's grafted

to the skin on my face & neck

fusing to bone & mandible

1:1 articulation simulating

real sincerity

      genuine empathy

I stopped removing it

a while back

choosing to keep up the facade

keeping in character

even behind closed doors

    between takes

perpetuating

the scam

the game

the fix

the never-ending

all-consuming charade

temporary

the thing about happiness

or sadness

is

         they are temporary

but madness...

      madness is forever

the Epitome of moxy

A man's worth

can be measured

by his capacity

to deal with the cards

he's been dealt.

Will his knees buckle

under the heavy load

or will he find the

strength to endure?

Will his back break under

the extreme pressure

that is almost guaranteed

on a daily basis?

Will he tuck his tail

between his legs

& run for cover

Or

will he align

his spine with

his knees

widen his stance

fill his heart

with resolve

& set his face as flint

eye to eye

& nose

to nose

with his hardships

refusing to give in

refusing

to surrender

until he sees the full realization

of his destiny unfold

before his very eyes.

That's the epitome of Moxy.

Joseph Fulkerson runs **Laughing Ronin Press** and is the author of ten books and chapbooks. His most recent, *The Electric Preacher,* was published through **Holy & intoxicated Publications.** He lives and works in the bourbon-soaked hills of Western Kentucky.

https://linktr.ee/josephfulkerson

Laughing Ronin Press, LLC
P.O. Box 234
Owensboro, Ky 42303
www.LaughingRoninPress.com